WISE WORDS

...from lessons learned.

> *"Wisdom is the reward you get for a lifetime of listening when you'd have preferred to talk."*
>
> DOUG LARSON

WAYNE KERR, DDS, MAGD

Ten Tips to the Top!
A primer for the successful dental practice.

When Life Needs a Sticky Note...
words of inspiration during challenging times

BIG Success for Small Business
...a primer for the entrepreneur

When Mom and Dad Need Help...
Caring for parents and loved ones.

TABLE *of* CONTENTS

PREFACE

As a young boy growing up in the fifties, I remember helping my dad fix things. Whether it was the car, the furnace, or the sink, my dad could fix it, and – by working beside him – I learned to fix things too.

We weren't well-to-do by any stretch of the imagination. We ate the heels of every loaf of bread, drank each gallon of milk to the last drop, and packed bologna and cheese sandwiches every Sunday afternoon for our school lunches for the coming week.

But when it came to fixing things, my dad had the finest tools money could buy. One day I asked Dad about that: "If we're not rich, how come you only buy Craftsman tools from Sears?" His answer was a moment which has stayed with me through more than six decades... He put his hand on my shoulder, looked me right in the eyes, and said, "Son, we're too poor to buy cheap. Buy quality tools, take care of them, and they will last a lifetime."

This book is a collection of some of the snippets of wisdom my father shared with me when I was a boy. A few of these may sound familiar to you. Others are phrased as only my father could have said them, but have universal meaning, and should be shared.

I hope my commentary is meaningful to you, and positively impacts your life. More importantly, I hope it reminds you of advice your own parents shared with you in your youth and that you may have passed on to your children. It's my belief that "sound advice" is always welcome, and that it's never too late to learn. After all, Life is a *Journey*, not a *Destination*. I wish you all the best.

— *Wayne Kerr, DDS, MAGD*

CHAPTER 1

Be Kind to Others

"You can be rich in spirit, kindness, love, and all those things that you can't put a dollar sign on."

DOLLY PARTON

BE KIND TO OTHERS

Dad launched our boat early on a Saturday morning in June at the public ramp in Cocoa Beach, and by late afternoon we docked at our overnight destination, Vero Beach. For my brother and me, the day had been a most excellent adventure. Dad had masterfully piloted the boat south while our neighbor, Bob Boyle, took pictures of the birds of the inland waterway for Life magazine.

While Dad and Mr. Boyle tied up the boat and arranged to have it refueled and docked for the night, we headed up the pier into town to find some ice cream. Vero Beach in 1966 was small and quaint, and we couldn't help but notice an interesting shop that was only open Wednesday and Saturday afternoons. We entered on a whim but were immediately rewarded by the sight of a magnificent array of unusual items. A pleasant woman welcomed us and asked if we were looking for anything special. When we advised her that we were from out of town and would head home the next day, she invited us to examine and enjoy the items in her shop and said, "Each piece tells a story."

As we strolled through the small store, it seemed that the painted eyes of a sculpture of a beautiful Polynesian girl followed me wherever I went. As I admired the piece, the shopkeeper commented that it was a memento from her honeymoon many years ago. But when I asked its price, I was disappointed to learn that it cost fifteen dollars which was ten dollars more than I had.

About that time a lady burst into the shop exclaiming that she had to have a gift right away, but before the shopkeeper could offer to help, her eyes focused on the lovely sculpture in my hands. She took it from me, put it on the counter and said, "I'll take this." Imagine my surprise when the woman behind the counter said, "I'm sorry, but it's already been sold."

After the lady stormed out in a huff, I reminded the shopkeeper that I only had five dollars and asked why she hadn't sold her the sculpture. She told me that the rude woman was a local and that she didn't care to sell her any treasures. "You see," she said, "The items in this shop are the collections of my lifetime. I don't have to sell any of them, but I enjoy spending a few hours each week meeting folks who appreciate them and can offer them a loving home."

Fifty-five years later, that sculpture still adorns my study and remains a constant reminder, not only of that great summer adventure with my older brother, but of the generosity of spirit of that shopkeeper. It's an important lesson in life, I believe, that kind-heartedness and courtesy never go out of style.

HOMEWORK ASSIGNMENT:

List three things that you can do in the coming week to show kindness to someone. And then do them!

1.

2.

3.

CHAPTER 2

Do Your Homework

*"An investment in knowledge
pays the best interest."*

BENJAMIN FRANKLIN

DO YOUR HOMEWORK

I grew up in central Florida in the fifties. Martin Marietta had just opened a major facility employing thousands, and new homes were under construction virtually everywhere. As a boy, it seemed there was always a sand pile to be played in.

I remember building a fort with a buddy in a vacant lot near our home. It grew late, and my dad yelled for me to come inside and do my homework. I can't remember my exact response, but I do recall spending two hours standing in the corner before bedtime. It seems that I told my father I didn't need an education, and that I was going to become a ditch digger. To this day, I do remember what Dad said: "Son. You can become anything you want, but, if you want to be more than a ditch digger one day, you'll need an education."

I got a similar piece of advice years later from Dad after I was offered the position of assistant manager for Gooding's Groceries the week before I left for college. Dad told me that the grocery business was an honorable business, and that I'd likely never have a better boss than Jim Gooding, but – if I wanted a college education – now was the time to go. If I got used to a paycheck, he said, I'd never go back to school.

I've always been grateful for that advice, as my collegiate education provided me with the opportunity to enjoy a career serving others while working with some of the finest people on the planet. I'd have been a really good ditch digger – maybe even one of the best – but owning and operating a small business as a general dentist has been incredibly fulfilling.

Taking my father's advice to heart, I never stopped learning, nor did I stop trying to improve my clinical skills for the welfare of my patients, or my management skills for the benefit of my teammates. That's what professionals do.

My childhood memories of playing in sand piles with my elementary school buddies are good ones, but my father's encouragement to "get an education" was most beneficial. As I write this, it's thirteen degrees outside, and our backyard pond is frozen over. Ditch-digging sounded pretty good as a boy, but – especially today – I'm thankful I heeded my father's advice!

HOMEWORK ASSIGNMENT:

Read a book on a topic of interest
to expand your knowledge or consider
enrolling in an online course to
enhance your skills.

CHAPTER 3

You Can't Do It All

"Choose Wisely."

FROM INDIANA JONES AND THE LAST CRUSADE

YOU CAN'T DO IT ALL

I loved junior high and high school and I loved learning. I enjoyed the challenges presented by a wide range of subjects, the opportunity to meet and make new friends, and especially the many school-sponsored activities. I played trombone in the band, lettered in multiple sports, served on the yearbook committee, and was a club president and student council member. Yeah, I loved it all.

There were some activities in which I could not participate, however, because they conflicted with my job at the grocery store. And there were times when activities and responsibilities collided head-on. As Dad often reminded me, "You can't do it all."

The most agonizing example of this conundrum occurred while in junior high. Thursday afternoon's band practice ended just as basketball practice began. Coach Dale Rider wouldn't excuse me for being late, but director John Stanley wouldn't allow me to leave fifteen minutes early. Since band was a year-round activity but basketball was seasonal, I never understood why neither would compromise so that I could do both!

In the end, I chose basketball even though I had to give up band. As a trombonist, it was fulfilling to contribute my part to those played by the other members of the band to make beautiful music for the spring concert. But, as one of the "starting five" on the basketball team, it was thrilling to be part of the action and to realize the impact I could have on the outcome of each game. And it certainly didn't hurt that beautiful cheerleaders were cheering me on!

Both in business and one's personal life, dozens of decisions are made each day. Some are easy, but some have consequences. Agreeing to chair our local hospital's Foundation, for example, required that I give up three hours of my clinical time each month to meet with its director. In short, I elected to give up some income to serve my community in, what was to me, a meaningful way.

A decision-making technique that has worked well for me is to review my daily, weekly, and monthly obligations to determine what free time I have before electing to take on anything new. I then evaluate the pros and cons associated with the decision. Finally, I ask myself the question, "How will this impact my family and/or my business?"

Don't overlook the importance of sharing the decision-making process with your family when appropriate, for you want to live your life in balance. Chronically living life out of balance leads to stress, poor health, and burnout. Don't let that happen to you. As the Knight in the movie *Indiana Jones and the Last Crusade* advised, "Choose wisely."

HOMEWORK ASSIGNMENT:

1. Make a list of your daily obligations.

2. Make a list of your weekly obligations.

3. Make a list of your weekend and family commitments.

4. Make a list of things you wish to do for yourself or add to your schedule.

5. Sit down with a monthly calendar and organize all responsibilities.

6. Identify your free time and enjoy it stress and guilt-free!

CHAPTER 4

Be a Team Player

*"Coming together is a beginning;
Keeping together is progress;
Working together is success."*

HENRY FORD

BE A TEAM PLAYER

My buddy, Jerry Miller, and I played basketball together as junior high school classmates. He was an inch taller and a good bit more muscular than me, and I quickly recognized that he could use his physical assets to break toward the basket and score! In fact, Jerry scored so often, I was recognized as the "All-County" assist leader at season's end. I wasn't really that good. I just anticipated when he would break for the basket and flipped him the ball at just the right moment. It was my good friend and teammate, that made me look like a star!

As a teen, Jerry made me look successful on the basketball court, but it was my employees – my professional teammates – that made me the success I was as a small-business owner and clinician. Unprepared as I was to operate a business, I quickly realized that I was only going to be as good as my team. I'd like to think that I won the "All County" assist leader each year I practiced, as I worked with my teammates to bring out the best in them while providing clinical excellence to those we served.

Like basketball, dentistry is a team sport. Unlike basketball, however, there is no point guard or "playmaker." Each member of the dental team is of equal value, and each must perform at the "top of their game" every day. And, when that happens, everyone wins. That's what teamwork is all about – recognizing the value each person brings to the team, and "flipping the ball to them" (like I did to my friend, Jerry) at just the right moment.

As a brilliant, innovative, and much-loved pediatrician, Dr. Jerry Miller, Jr. served thousands of children, saved numerous lives, and contributed significantly to the science of pediatrics. And, throughout his marvelous career, he always credited his success to others. A true star, whether playing the game of basketball or playing the game of life, Jerry remained humble, and always recognized the true value of a teammate.

I know I was a much better employer and far more successful as a small-business owner because I learned how to be a team player and a good teammate early in life. And that's a valuable lesson for us all at any age. Thanks, Jerry.

HOMEWORK ASSIGNMENT:

Reconnect with a friend, classmate, or mentor and let them know by a phone call, email, or hand-written note just how much they have meant to you.

CHAPTER 5

Life Isn't Fair

"What are stumbling blocks and defeat to the weak and vacillating are but stepping-stones to victory to the determined soul."

O. S. MARDEN

LIFE ISN'T FAIR

It seems that, at any early age, my older brother and I got into trouble either for something we did, but shouldn't have done, or something we didn't do but got blamed for by our little sister. And, each time we were punished, we proclaimed that "that's not fair!" Dad always responded with the question, "Whoever said life is fair?"

Mom didn't bake much, so getting to pick out a birthday cake from the local bakery was a *really big* deal. For my fifth birthday, I chose a white cake covered with chocolate butter cream icing. The single candle was in the shape of a "5."

The table was set, and the cake was placed right in the middle, just across from my chair. I remember carrying my glass of milk to the table and holding it by both hands so I wouldn't spill it. I reached up to the table and pushed my glass as far onto it as I could. A minute later I returned holding my plate of spaghetti and meat sauce and pushed it up on the table as well.

Unfortunately, my plate knocked over the glass of milk, soiling the heirloom tablecloth and soaking my cake. As I reached up to grab the glass, I let go of my plate, which wasn't *quite* on the table yet. Predictably, it flipped upside down and landed on the dining room chair which had just been recovered by my mom and grandmother the week before.

Faster than you can say "Jumpin' Jack Flash," my birthday was over. I was sent to my room without dinner, without cake, without a party, and without presents. Whoever said, "Life is fair?"

After turning six, I was invited to fish with my dad and grandfather on Lake Maggiore in St. Petersburg, Florida. Pop had a small metal fishing boat which we toted to the lake and launched into the water. And that was when Pop handed me my very own Zebco push-button rod and reel! I was thrilled!

The August day was hot and humid, without clouds or a breeze, the fish weren't biting, and the 12' pram became hot to the touch. By late morning I was thirsty and set my brand-new rod and reel on the seat of the boat to grab an ice cold Frostie root beer from the Styrofoam cooler. Being six, it never occurred to me to first reel in my hook. As chance would have it, a fish took my bait – *and* my rod and reel. *Gone, over the side!*

Unable to fish, I became the "deck hand." Told to "throw out the anchor," I did. How was I supposed to know it wasn't tied to the boat? Too late, we witnessed the last few feet of anchor line slide into the water. *Gone, over the side!!*

Later, Dad asked me to grab the bait bucket, a perforated metal container which was dragged through the water behind the boat. After Dad grabbed a shiner to rebait his hook, he told me to "throw it back in the water." I did as I was told but failed to put it back into its outer holder first. It sank immediately. *Gone, over the side!!!*

What should have been a grand adventure for a six-year-old kid fishing with his dad and Pop ended in disaster. I was crushed. *And* I'd lost my very own Zebco rod and reel that I had for less than a day. After we got home, I was sent to bed *with* a sunburn, but *without* dinner. (My grandmother "smuggled" in a bowl of mac and cheese and a glass of milk to my bedroom when she came to kiss me goodnight.) Whoever said, "Life is fair?"

Reflecting on these boyhood experiences reminds me of just how fortunate I was to learn early on that life really isn't fair, for it prepared me for reality. Life is filled with adversity, and it's important to develop the necessary resilience to overcome the challenges that come our way each day.

I might have missed my fifth birthday party and ruined a boyhood summertime adventure, but I learned a valuable lesson from those painful experiences that has helped me overcome many of life's challenges. And for that, I'm most grateful.

HOMEWORK ASSIGNMENT:

Reflect on some of your own experiences when you were treated unfairly. How did you respond? What did you learn? More importantly, if you're a parent, have you shared experiences with your child or children to help them cope when treated unfairly?

CHAPTER 6

Keep Your Nose Clean

"Never borrow trouble."

J. C. KERR, JR.

KEEP YOUR NOSE CLEAN

I was fourteen years old and had a crush on a girl who lived just down the street. She was blonde, athletic, and a year older than me. She had the cutest little upturned nose and wore a constant smile on her face. In short, I was smitten, and wanted to get to know her better.

The good news is that I was taking ninth grade science as an eighth grader, and we were classmates. Wahoo! The bad news is that, like Charlie Brown and the girl with the curly red hair, I couldn't bring myself to talk to her.

As the fall semester neared its end, however, I hatched a plan! Summoning all the courage I had, I stammered the suggestion that, since we were neighbors, we could study for the final exam together. I was dumbfounded when she agreed. We made a date for 10:00 Saturday morning at her house.

I finished my yard work early, showered, dressed, and slicked down my hair with a little dab of my brother's Brylcreem. I wore my best pair of plaid shorts and my favorite Banlon shirt. Yeah, I thought I was about as cool as an eighth grader could get.

I'll never forget that, as I walked out the front door for my date, my dad stopped me with a hand on my shoulder. As I turned to face him, he said, "Son, keep your nose clean!" And, I thought to myself, "What does *that* mean? Do I need to blow my nose?"

That thought stayed with me the entire time it took me to walk down the street to my classmate's house. It bothered me so much that I was looking up at my nose in the reflection of her front door's glass window to make sure that it was clean when she opened the door. "What are you doing?" she asked. Red-faced with embarrassment, I told her that I wanted to make sure my nose was clean. And, with that, she burst into laughter and said "It is! Come in!"

It was years later when the real meaning of my father's words finally hit me. He wasn't talking about my appearance, he was talking about my behavior. "Keep your nose clean" means *stay out of trouble!* And that's sound advice for any age.

HOMEWORK ASSIGNMENT:

In addition to not doing things we shouldn't do, it's equally important that we avoid putting ourselves in situations which might not turn out well. Zig Ziglar reminded us that much of who we become as a person is determined by who we spend our time with and what we put into our mind. If you're a parent, have a conversation with your kids about choosing friends wisely and avoiding trouble.

CHAPTER 7

Always Do
Your Best

"The only certain means of success is
to render more and better service than
is expected of you, no matter what
your task may be."

OG MANDINO

ALWAYS DO YOUR BEST

Any successful business, including a dental practice, is built on customer service and satisfaction. Imagine how a business and its reputation can be harmed by an employee who doesn't care about the customer or their satisfaction.

Recently my wife and I contracted to replace an aging sliding glass door to our patio. The installer arrived an hour later than planned but seemed pleasant enough as he began his work. When we expressed surprise that he was alone, he informed us that he'd been installing doors for seventeen years and didn't need anyone's help. Hmmm...

Removing our old door gave him unexpected trouble, set him further behind schedule, and seemed to sour his mood. We watched with growing concern as he crow-barred the door from its framing causing unexpected (and unnecessary) damage to our home. During this process, he repeatedly called his next customer to assure them he'd be there soon.

In his haste to finish, he failed to fully square the door frame, improperly installed the accessory lock, failed to adjust the latch, and left a gaping hole above the door that allowed the winter wind to whistle in. Worse, the door only opened about eighteen inches! Although a cold afternoon rain was forecast, he ignored the hole, packed up his gear, and told us that the door would become easier to open in time. Good bye!

My wife and I spent three days resolving the problems he created. We sealed the hole and insulated the entire installation with foam before the rain arrived, then reinstalled the accessory lock, handle, and alarm, adjusted the latch, caulked and painted the outdoor trim, and sanded, stained, and installed the indoor trim. Although we've successfully made our new door functional, our experience with this company and its employee was absolutely abysmal. If I had employed a person with his attitude for seventeen years (or even *one*), I'd never have had a successful practice, nor would my patients have been properly served. I can't help but think that it's time for this gentleman to move on to something else, for if this is his idea of service excellence and giving his best, it should be "quittin' time" for him!

HOMEWORK ASSIGNMENT:

Identify vendors or service providers that you tolerate in spite of poor service.

Identify alternatives to replace them. Why pay someone for less than their best?

CHAPTER 8

Plan Ahead

> *"All our dreams can come true if we have the courage to pursue them."*
>
> WALT DISNEY

PLAN AHEAD

Author's note: Ironically, this blog was my last post for 2019. Who knew that even carefully made plans can disappear in the blink of an eye?

When our kids were young, we enjoyed many adventures in a small RV. I'd plan detailed itineraries using a few AAA maps and a copy of National Geographic's Guide to the National Parks. Sometimes we'd be on the road for a week or more, just exploring the incredible beauty of this great land. Most often, however, we took advantage of long holiday weekends to visit family in Florida and North Carolina.

One favorite trip became an annual event. We'd drive to Pensacola, Florida for the Memorial Day weekend and stay with a relative who lived on the beach. The water was always warm, the sand pristine, the fresh grilled fish delicious, and time together wonderful.

One year, however, circumstances beyond our control prevented us from going, and we were all disappointed. Yes, we'd miss the water, the sand, the food, and time with relatives, but we'd still enjoy the holiday together as a family. And then a crazy thought occurred to me.... What if we *pretended* that we went?

With a truck load of builder's sand, I converted our backyard pool and patio area into "Pensacola Beach." After spreading the sand appropriately, I put up the big umbrella, broke out the beach chairs, iced down a cooler of soft drinks, and grilled fresh caught salmon. We swam in the pool, batted a beach ball, and played favorite songs by the Beach Boys on a portable CD player. It wasn't quite the same, of course, but feeling the sand between our toes created the desired illusion that we were beachside and added to the air of festivity!

We can't always do that which we wish to do, but that doesn't mean we should abandon a dream. Want to drive the Pacific Coast Highway, visit New England in the fall, hike Arches National Park, or take a trip on Route 66? Stop wishing! Sit down with a pencil and pad of paper and start planning. List all the reasons why you don't think you can pull it off, and then write down all the reasons why you *can*. Think creatively, find ways to eliminate the obstacles, and – next year – make it happen. If you don't, no one else will! Happy trails...

HOMEWORK ASSIGNMENT:

1. Sit down with your family and brainstorm a fun trip or activity for next year.

2. Establish a budget.

3. Identify the dates.

4. Make reservations (review cancellation policies).

5. Build excitement: post a picture of your destination on the refrigerator.

CHAPTER 9

Keep Your Chin Up

*"Any fact facing us is not as important
as our attitude toward it, for that
determines our success or failure."*

NORMAN VINCENT PEALE

KEEP YOUR CHIN UP

Author's note: I was disappointed and discouraged when I failed to make the final cut for my high school basketball team my junior year. Predictably, my dad said, "Son, keep your chin up!" And that's been great advice throughout my life. As my own family and close friends have been adversely impacted by the pandemic of 2020, I've tried to move forward with a positive attitude and "keep my chin up." In the face of great challenges, a local business owner and friend of mine did more than that... She reinvented her business and inspired her team to keep hope alive

My friend, Jennifer, owns The Sketching Pad, a favorite pre-pandemic hangout for artists of all ages. For many years, Jennifer and her exceptionally creative team have hosted all manner of in-house art classes, painting parties, special events, and the all-important "paint by wine" event for adult dabblers.

Like so many small, family owned enterprises, The Sketching Pad suffered large financial losses when businesses were forced to close to "flatten the viral curve." Through innovation, "outside the box thinking," and teamwork, however, no one at The Sketching Pad lost their job during this challenging time.

Using their colorful and inviting web site and the creativity of the entire team, The Sketching Pad launched "paint at home" projects, including new ones each week, and marketed their numerous products to all former clients. And, to ensure that any novice could succeed, they produced more than sixty online videos that coincide with each project to provide step by step instructions. Amazing!

When small businesses reopened here in Georgia, The Sketching Pad made in-person instruction possible again by using smaller tables with only two chairs at each, about eight feet apart. Jennifer and her team wear face shields, maintain appropriate distance, and have hand sanitizer available before and after you enter their studio.

The greatest thing about this American success story, however, is that Jennifer and her coworkers never allowed the pandemic to steal their dreams or cause them to lose hope. Anyone walking into their studio is immediately struck by their warm greeting and genuine smiles, high energy, and positive attitudes!

At a time when so many have sacrificed so much for the good of others, it's important to remember that focusing on solutions, working toward a better day, and keeping hope in our hearts is precisely what we need to do. And Jennifer and her wonderful team have reminded me of that! Thanks so much, and best wishes for your continuing success! (For awesome art, visit www.thesketchingpad.com).

HOMEWORK ASSIGNMENT:

Write down the challenges you currently face and identify possible solutions. Reach out to family and friends for help and focus on the positive steps you might take to resolve each issue. Keep moving forward and keep hope in your heart.

CHAPTER 10

Celebrate the Victories!

"Allow yourself small victories.
Don't deny giving yourself credit for
accomplishing something, no matter how
insignificant it might seem at the time."

LIVELIFEHAPPY.COM

CELEBRATE THE VICTORIES!

During an early morning walk through a local state park, I encountered an elderly woman walking with a cane. As I greeted her, she asked "Where is this place that you can go to see the rocks?" I pointed to a nearby boardwalk and said, "It's here." And then I complemented her for her achievement as it was obvious to me that she'd walked a long way with difficulty to arrive at this location.

She surprised me when she started complaining. "They told me this was easy! They told me this was just a half-mile! It's more than a mile, and it was all uphill!" I smiled in return, and said, "You made it, and it's all downhill on the way back. Enjoy." As I departed, I heard her begin complaining all over again to a couple of people who were leaving the viewing area. "They told me this was easy....."

As I continued my walk, I savored the lovely wildflowers, enjoyed hearing the song of a mockingbird, watched two bunnies scamper away, and picked a few wild blackberries. But my thoughts kept returning to the elderly woman. She should have celebrated her achievement, walking more than a mile with an elevation gain of over 300 feet with a cane. But she chose instead to complain.

Oddly, this experience reminded me of dentistry. Even on a well-planned day, meeting the needs of those for whom you care can be stressful and exhausting. It's easy to complain that the morning schedule ran into lunch, and that two more emergencies were "worked into" the afternoon schedule forcing everyone to work late. I get it.

But successfully serving each patient with excellence is cause for celebration! Why not share just a moment to do so as the patient is dismissed? Thank the patient for the opportunity to care for them, complement your hygienist or chairside assistant for a job well done, and celebrate each victory! Doing so, completely changes the day's "narrative" and adds joy to every day.

When I reached the mile marker that was my turn around point, I reversed course and headed back to my car. Ironically, the elderly woman I'd met earlier was just returning to the path from the overlook as I approached the boardwalk. "Wasn't it pretty, I asked?" "It was just a pile of rocks," she replied. "And now I have to walk all the way back."

Hmmm... I think she missed the opportunity to celebrate. Don't let that happen to you.

HOMEWORK ASSIGNMENT:

1. Write down an event that you celebrated yesterday.

2. Write down something that you celebrated today and share with family.

3. Write down an opportunity to celebrate tomorrow - and celebrate!

The Stuff That Matters

*"It's not what we have in our life, but
who we have in our life that counts."*

J. M. LAURENCE

THE STUFF THAT MATTERS

Author's note: This modified blog was posted in December, 2017, five years after I had retired from full-time clinical practice. Although it's written from the relaxed perspective of a retiree, it reminds one of the importance of thankful reflection throughout a lifetime.

Recently I spent a day shredding sensitive documents, including old payroll and 401(k) reports. Each record was meticulously organized and carefully preserved. As the pages disintegrated before my eyes, I was reminded of the sheer volume of work required by a small-business owner, and the growing complexity of it all. Add in the typical "year-end" tasks and the desire by patients to utilize available third-party benefits, and December can be a bit overwhelming.

Having said that, it is my belief that it is more important than ever to take time for quiet reflection during this busy season, and think about the stuff that really matters to you, whatever that may be. Revisit those experiences which brought you joy, let go of past disappointments you can't change, and fill your heart and mind with those successes which positively impacted the lives of others!

As I reflect upon 2017, I'm filled with an enormous sense of gratitude. It's been my privilege to continue to contribute to the education of current and future dental professionals across this land. I've benefitted greatly from the wisdom and guidance of others who add value to my life. My wife and I have been blessed with another grandchild, and members of our immediate family were spared significant damage, destruction, or harm from both hurricane Irma in Florida and the wildfires of California.

I've spent this year reading, writing, teaching, and studying, free from the demands and schedules of a busy practice. Enjoying walking and biking in the nearby state park has become a daily event. Family projects have kept me engaged and physically active, and I am reminded of how fortunate I am to enjoy the good health that lets me do these things.

And, after years of being pet free, little Gundry joined our family in June. It wasn't an easy decision, but it certainly proved to be a good one, as our adorable Shichon has filled our hearts with joy, and brings us reasons to laugh throughout the day.

As the year-end approaches, reflect on that for which you're thankful and fills your heart with peace. Cherish time with family and loved ones and celebrate those simple things that make you smile.

In the chaos of December, focus on the stuff that matters most and let the little things around you bring you happiness and joy. May your new year be blessed as never before....

HOMEWORK ASSIGNMENT:

Count your blessings - and live your life
with the balance necessary to ensure
that you get to enjoy them.

ABOUT THE AUTHOR

Since 1994, Wayne has been sharing his wit and wisdom with students, educators, and dental professionals across the U. S. and Canada. Although he generally speaks on scientific topics or practice management, his presentations on "Life Skills" seem to resonate with audiences everywhere. His books, *"When Mom and Dad Need Help,"* and *"When Life Needs a Sticky Note"* were written in response to almost universal interest.

This book, *"Wise Words from Lessons Learned,"* was inspired by the many snippets of wisdom offered to Wayne as a youth by his father, J. C. Kerr, Jr. Many of these words of advice contributed to his core values and character, and it is his belief that, by sharing, others can benefit as well.

As a professional, Wayne earned numerous honors, including Fellowship in both the American and International Colleges of Dentistry, the Pierre Fauchard Academy, as an Honored Fellow of the Georgia Dental Association, Mastership in the Academy of

General Dentistry, and as a recipient of the Academy's Life Long Learning and Service Recognition Award.

As a community volunteer, Wayne has been recognized as Professional, Citizen, Volunteer, and Small-business Person of the Year. Additionally, he was honored by the Georgia Institute of Technology with its presentation of the Dean Griffin Community Service Award. Working with other community leaders, Wayne helped found a clinic for the indigent providing free dental and medical services.

Retired from clinical care, Wayne's passion is to shorten the learning curve to success for other dentists and their team members. He is an Adjunct Associate Professor for the University of Alabama's School of Dentistry, helps prepare dental hygiene students for their National Board Exam (www.dhseminars.com) , speaks on a variety of topics for major dental meetings, and posts a monthly blog called kerrthoughts. Archived blogs are available at www.kerrspeak.com as well as other resources for practice building, or text the word kerrspeak to 22828 to access a link to sign up for his commentary on the first Thursday of every month. Contact Wayne by email at wayne@kerrspeak.com.

Made in the USA
Columbia, SC
14 December 2024